She Who Rises

A Testament to Unapologetic Womanhood

Meera Juneja

India | USA | UK

Copyright © Meera Juneja
All Rights Reserved.

This book has been self-published with all reasonable efforts taken to make the material error-free by the author. No part of this book shall be used, reproduced in any manner whatsoever without written permission from the author, except in the case of brief quotations embodied in critical articles and reviews.

The Author of this book is solely responsible and liable for its content including but not limited to the views, representations, descriptions, statements, information, opinions, and references ["Content"]. The Content of this book shall not constitute or be construed or deemed to reflect the opinion or expression of the Publisher or Editor. Neither the Publisher nor Editor endorse or approve the Content of this book or guarantee the reliability, accuracy, or completeness of the Content published herein and do not make any representations or warranties of any kind, express or implied, including but not limited to the implied warranties of merchantability, fitness for a particular purpose.

The Publisher and Editor shall not be liable whatsoever...

Made with ❤ on the BookLeaf Publishing Platform
www.bookleafpub.in
www.bookleafpub.com

Dedication

To the women who have preceded me and those who will follow.
May our tales live on forever.

Preface

During the course of my life, I have gradually been learning one thing: patriarchy is not merely a tale from the past but rather the very condition of life. It is the very existence of society, so to speak, that is reflected in the way girls were told to behave and even talk and dream, so much so that finally, when they are allowed to be themselves, they are already deep into the feminine script. Boys are the ones who are praised, and girls were the ones who are taught. It is there in the school where crying is considered as something only a girl would do, while a boy will act all tough and masculine. It is in the workplaces where pleasantness in men and women meant different things, the former being power and the latter being labelled as attitude.

We are told that the modern world is ours, where women have rights, choices, and voices. But the truth is that every little move we made towards freedom is accompanied by a whisper reminding us of the unseen barriers.

This book is not born out of bitterness, but rather of understanding. Understanding of how silently patriarchy is still with us, hidden under the guise of custom, care, custody, or 'just how it is.' These poems are the result of the common experiences when women notice the veil being lifted and the truth being uncovered. From the breaths we take when we are cut off. From the anger we suppress when our hurt is denied. From the satisfaction we get every time a woman, any woman, gets a bit higher than the world had expected.

Not only is this book a compilation of poems, but also a proof of enlightenment. It represents the silent realisation of the whole female population who raised their voice. Unlocking the invisible strings attached to our lives through one's own insight made us relate to each other, and it gave us the courage to speak up about our worth.

Acknowledgements

This book is for my mom, my first teacher, my first friend, the woman who taught me to rise and gave me the strength to face the world. Mumma, even though I don't say it often, I love you more than words can ever describe.

This book also serves as a tribute not only to the women who went before us but also to the women of today who are still fighting the same battles in various arenas such as homes, offices, streets and even within their own selves.

1. Excessive in Being

They remarked that she was excessive.
Excessive in decibels,
excessive in the unleashing of her wildness,
Excessive in her expression
"Tone it down," they said, while decreasing their voices,
as if she were something that needed to be confined.

She never attempted to occupy space; she merely did it.
She entered, and the atmosphere was not the same,
Not because she sought notice,
But because of the nonexistence of her fear of being.

Her laughter? The kind that was heard prior to her being seen.
Unrestrained, genuine, alive.
Some liked it, others disapproved,
As if it was a crime.

"Be still," they advised her.
"Become more like them."

But she never understood why the smallness
Was the condition for being accepted
and if quietness was indeed a mark of grace.

She made the effort, oh, she did! to fit into their little boxes,
To smooth out the rough parts of her being.
But it was like wearing a poorly fitted coat
Uncomfortable, oppressive, wrong.

She was never trying to rebel.
She simply possessed the gift of listening to her inner self.
She would dance when the moment came,
Raise her voice when there was a matter of importance.

And when they said, "You're too much,"
She ceased to apologise.
She ceased to clarify.
Because one can never tell what if, just what if
She was not too much, indeed.

Perhaps the world was just too little for a person who wouldn't settle for living halfway.

2. The Mirror Doesn't Make The Girl

She scrolls.
Frame after flawless frame,
waists snatched, skin blurred,
"Hot girl summer" with a matching filter.
They call it beauty.
They call it goals.
But who decided perfection had to come with editing tools?

She stands before the mirror,
A thousand voices in her head:
"Too short."
"Too plain."
"Too real."
And yet, too much to be ignored.

Because the mirror doesn't make the girl.
And neither does a screen.
She's not here to be curated.

She's here to be seen.
They said fashion is for the flawless,
but she knows better.

She wears combat boots with courage.
Her eyeliner is sharp enough to cut bias.
And her outfit?
A rebellion stitched in bold seams and brighter dreams.

No, she won't contour her culture,
Crop her curves,
or hide behind hashtags like #blessed
when she's battling just to be herself.

Her body isn't a billboard.
Her face isn't a filter.
Her worth isn't built in likes,
but in the freedom to wear her story,
no cuts, no apologies, and totally her own.

So let the world watch.
She'll strut through the chaos,
with her truth tucked in her pocket
and a glare strong enough to untrain generations.

Because the girl makes the fashion.
The fashion doesn't make the girl.

And the mirror?
It's lucky just to reflect her fire.

3. Cry, Laugh, Conquer

They tell me,
"Be strong, be tough, don't cry, stand tall."
But the moment I do, they say.
"Uff, so cold, so harsh, why no warmth at all?"

Oh, so respect is a game, and the rules are bizarre.
If I'm soft, I'm weak. If I'm bold, I've gone too far.
If I smile, I'm 'too nice.' If I frown, I'm 'too rude.'
If I lead, I'm 'bossy.' If I listen, I 'lack the attitude.'

"You must dress sharp! Power suits! No frills, no bows!"
But when I do, "Oh dear, why so serious though?"
If I wear pink, "That's childish, stay away from the glitter."
But in black, "Madam, why so bitter?"

If I speak my mind, "She's too aggressive, too loud."
If I stay silent, "She's mysterious... or maybe just proud?"
If I hug too much, "Too clingy, not independent."
If I hug too little, "Cold, distant... so inconsistent."

They say I should be ambitious, chase dreams without fear,
but when I rise too fast, "Oh, she's insincere."
If I balance work and home, I'm a "superwoman, "
If I focus on me, I'm "selfish," or worse, a "loon."

You see the problem? The endless disguise?
The hoops I must jump through just to be "wise"?
Why should I fit into a mould built for men,
when my power, my grace, is already a ten?

I don't need to "man up" to earn your salute;
I'll conquer in heels or maybe a cute boot.
Not every leader needs a deep, roaring voice.
Some rule the world with a laugh, and that's their choice!

I can cry without shame, I can roar without guilt,
I can wear sequins or suits, or a soft pastel quilt.
I can be a mother, a sister, a CEO, a queen;
I can be all the things they said I shouldn't have been.

So, keep your "act like a man" advice on a shelf.
Respect me, my way, as I am, MYSELF.
For I am enough in my softness and my fire,
I don't need to shrink, conform, or retire.

I am loud, I am gentle, I am rage and delight,
I am the dawn breaking boldly after the night.
And if you can't handle all that I am and can be,
Step aside, there's space in this world for me.

4. Motherhood ain't the mandate

Oh, society, please go ahead and take a seat, let's talk it over,
You are reeling in the past like a dusty old hat
"Motherhood's her righteousness," you declare with pride,
But sweetheart, that narrative is old and lame

When a woman comes into your view, what is the first question?
"Married? Kids?" It is indeed your favourite querying task.
Her aspirations, ambitions, and her blazing trail?
Oh no, that is of secondary in your story.

But let me serve you the hot and fresh tea:
Not every woman's womb is to be plotted as a trophy.
She is not a nursery, a life-exuding machine;
She is a goddess, a powerful and irresistible nature.

Women differ in their conquests;
one might go to the peak, while another might write a book,
The third one might chase the dream,
while the other one might be perfecting her cooking looks.
Motherhood is a choice, not the only mandate,
So stop turning it into her one-way dress.

"Biological clock!" you loudly decree,
Like she is a bomb ticking at thirty-three!
But hey, dear, here comes the news; she decides how fast or slow she goes,
Her value is not confined to wombs or some race.

5. Power In Softness

People consider me to be gentle,
say that I am too soft,
As if being nice is a quality that will make you lose.
Like if you don't shout, if you don't ask for something,
You'll be left behind, unseen, unheard.

They are friendly to me as if I am not aware,
As if I don't understand what their opinion about me is.
"She's too nice," they say very quietly,
"She will not resist, she will just surrender."

But they are unaware of the wars I win,
the unvoiced ones, the covert ones.
The burden I take up without making a fuss,
The way I get up when I have been beaten.

I have stayed quiet when conversations could break,
I have opted for peace when I could have been violent.
I have been the peaceful person in someone's trouble,
I have protected their heat and given them comfort.

Although people are making a wrong interpretation of this as a weakness,
They think that if one is kind, then one must be timid.
Like if you are patient, then you will never lose it,
Like if you love, then you will never hit back.

But I am not powerless; I was never so.
I just don't engage in ways they would like.
I do not have to yell to be heard,
I do not have to be angry to create a spark.

I am aware of my power, I am aware of my value,
And I will not take the world for the first one to acknowledge it.
So let them have whatever opinion they want to have about me,
I will be silently victorious in my battles.

6. Parathas, Not Patriarchy

"Girls should learn to cook," they say with a grin,
"Or how will you manage when husbands walk in?"
I roll my eyes and try not to laugh,
"Ever heard of YouTube? Or men who can craft?"

If food had a gender, imagine the scene,
Would burgers be "manly" and cupcakes a queen?
Would grills be for dads, all smoky and charred,
While moms just stir pots and watch from afar?

But step into any roadside stall,
Where the oil sizzles and spices call,
You'll see men flipping parathas with flair,
And women tossing noodles high in the air.

Gordon Ramsay shouts in his five-star space,
No one tells him, "Go home, know your place."
So why do we still hear, time and again
That the kitchen belongs to only some men?

Cooking's a skill, like dancing or art,
It's about passion, not some assigned part.
So grab that spatula, taste and explore,
Because food is for everyone, now and forevermore

7. Beyond The Cloth

They glance, they whisper, they shake their heads,
like what I wear is a book they haven't read.
A hoodie means I'm up to no good.
A hijab? Oh no, "she's misunderstood."

However, let me ask you, what is it that irritates you so?
Is it the textile or the truth
that I am aware ofCompletely who I am, what I want to wear,
And I don't want your criticism, I really don't mind.

"She must be a victim of oppression!" Oh, not this again,
I swear I've heard better takes from pigeons in Spain.
You see the cloth, I see my choice,
A choice that is mine, my own damn voice.

"But what if she's forced?", What if she's not?
What if I *like* this, ever thought of that?
What if your worries are just too loud?
What if I'm comfy, feeling safe and proud?

"Oh, but security!", Oh, that's real cute,
Yet bikers and skiers don't get the boot.
Scarves and hoods are a problem, you say?
But helmets and masks? No issues today?

Funny how "freedom" is all well and good,
Until a woman stands where you never could.
I dress for myself, not for your gaze,
Not for approval, not for praise.

So perhaps simply so, drink your own tea,
And let me wear what gives me strength.
A sweatshirt, a headscarf, loose or snug,
My body, my right, my life, my demand.

8. No. Period.

They say, *"But why?"* with a puzzled face,
Like my refusal needs a courtroom case.
Boy, let me spell it, clear and true,
N. O. That's all for you.

You beg, you plead, you act all stunned,
But honey, my "no" ain't here for fun.
It's not a maybe, not a test,
Not a quiz for you to guess.

Oh, you think I owe you a reason?
Baby, that logic's out of season.
My words aren't riddles to be undone,
It's a full stop, discussion's none.

You say, *"Convince me, make me see,"*
Oh sweetheart, that ain't on me.
I ain't here to soothe your pride,
Or keep your fragile ego alive.

So take that ego, pack it tight,
And walk away, *you'll be alright.*
'Cause my "no" stands tall and free,
Without a warranty.

And if that bruises your ego,
Well, darling, *I just won.*

9. Redefining The Summit

We do not need to your standards,
Neither do we want to be where you are.
Mankind does not represent the top,
And the standards of our searching are not him.

Neither do we say your thing back,
Nor are we branches that are twisted to carry your name.
The rights that we claim are not to copy your rights,
But to let our own open up.

Equality is not your privilege to grant,
Nor are you to set the limit of our ascendance by your permission.
We do not want to play your role,
But to write our own, from the deepest part of us and with love.

You are not the utmost of what is whole,
Not the prototype of every objective.

We do not want to take over your crown,
But rather, to make our own be of great fame.

We are the fire, the storm, the ocean,
Unapologetic, daring, and liberated.
We do not come up to make you our relatives,
our strength is deeply anchored in us.

So do not impose the necessity of fitting your model on us,
We are the yet-untold narratives.
Claiming rights is not about drawing comparisons,
But about asserting the area that has been there all along.

Humanity does not have just one face,
And its beauty cannot be confined by a single gender.
We do not rise to reflect the male image,
We rise to be alive, once and again.

10. Judged for Existing

A woman who rises, who dares to speak,
Is called "too much," "too bold," "too weak."
A man who does the very same,
Is hailed a hero, crowned with fame.

If she dresses bright, or dares to shine,
They whisper, judge, and draw a line.
But when a man steps into view,
His charm is praised, his choices "true."

A woman who sheds a tear in pain
Is told her strength is all in vain.
But when a man's heart starts to show,
They call it courage, let emotions flow.

When she commands, with vision clear,
They label her "harsh," instill their fear.
But when he leads with firm control,
He's seen as worthy of the role.

Why must the world draw different frames,
One dressed in glory, the other in blame?
The same vivid fire, the same intense spark,
only that she is imprisoned while he glorifies himself.

It's time to unmask this hidden guise,
Where judgment falls with blinded eyes.
Let truth be louder than worn-out lies,
And let every woman, unshaken, rise.

11. Suggested by Society

"Why do women..."
...talk so much?
...stay silent?
...complain?
...not leave?
...want rights if they already have them?

The search bar blinks,
like an eye, wide with suspicion,
as if womanhood were a mystery to be solved,
a glitch in nature that needs explaining.

"Are girls allowed..."
...to become pilots?
...to travel alone?
...to stay out late?
...to have dreams bigger than marriage?
...to be more successful than men?

Each question is a cage made of letters,

typed by fingers that never typed,
"Are boys allowed to be free?"

"Should wives..."
...work if husbands earn enough?
...keep their last name?
...ask before spending money?
...be punished for disobedience?

The internet does not lie;
it simply reflects
the truths we try to hide in daylight.
And in between every search,
is an unnamed woman,
who typed the question herself,
not because she doubted her worth,
but because the world taught her to.

She searched for permission
in pixels and prediction bars,
trying to decode how to exist
without being called *too much*,
or *too little*.

She never typed,
"Can I just be?"
But maybe,

that is the search she carries
in the quiet rebellion of her heart,
ready to be typed.
Ready to be seen.

12. Silencing The Scroll

If my body had a comment section,
it wouldn't be loud,
it would be constant.
A scrolling feed of people deciding
who I am
before I ever get the chance.

Some comments arrive disguised as compliments:
"You'd be perfect if you just lost a little..."
"Such a pretty face, don't waste it."
They place hunger in my hands
and call it *self-improvement.*

Others pretend to be concerned,
They wrap their fear in softness,
but it still scrapes when it touches my skin.

Even silence has a voice in this section,
the way eyes scan me in a room,
as if I am an exhibit

they forgot to approve.

There is no "like" button for breathing,
but somehow they still evaluate it.

And yet,
in the quiet hours,
when I am alone
with no mirrors, no watchers,
no flashing opinions,
my body speaks back to me
in a voice softer than any judgment:

*"You have survived everything.
You have carried me through storms.
Why must you ask strangers
for permission
to exist in peace?"*

For once,
I do not scroll.
I do not refresh.
I simply listen.
And in that moment,
with the world still whispering,
I whisper louder:

"Comments closed.
I'm finally home."

13. Lessons In Control

Welcome to a miraculous classroom,
where girls take experiment to the next level in terms of fashion,
and boys are unadulterated talented scholars.

She has a pencil skirt on, what a disaster!
"Sit up straight, alter the style that you hem,
do not draw your fellow students' attention with your legs."
He is in a hoodie that is three times larger than his size,
and all at once he becomes an artist hidden behind the cloth.

Her ponytail swings once - red alert!
His messy hair defies gravity - genius at work.

Pencils behind ears: girls - criminal accessory,
boys - symbol of readiness.

She raises her hand politely -

"Too loud, too bossy, too ambitious."
He slouches and blurts the same answer -
"Brilliant, young man, you inspire us all!"

Her shoes click - alarm bells. His sneakers squeak -
music of leadership.

And when the bell rings, girls walk quietly in measured
steps, boys sprint out like free radicals.

But fear not, young ladies,
for someday your pencil will become a sword,
your skirt a suit of armour,
and the dress code will finally have to learn that brains
cannot be hemmed."

14. Unbound

There was a time when corsets weren't just fashion,
They were rules stitched in satin, pain disguised as passion.
Girls stood still while laces pulled tight,
Ribs crushed, breaths stolen, yet still, they smiled polite.

"Be smaller," they said. "Be softer, be less."
So she held her breath and hid her stress.
The world wanted her neat, dainty, and thin,
So she tucked her dreams and fire within.

But times changed, and so did she.
Now, when she grabs a corset, it's not to break free,
It's to feel strong, to stand up tall,
To say, *I own this body, bones, curves, and all.*

She laces it up with steady hands,
Not to impress but to take a stand.
"This isn't for you," her bold eyes gleam,
"I wear this because *I love me.*"

It no longer steals her breath away,
It reminds her to breathe fire every day.
Once a chain, now a choice,
And this time, it's her own voice.

15. Vocal Fire

How dare you tell me to stay quiet?
To choke my words in a world so biased?
This tongue was born to shape my truth,
Not to bend or break for your brittle roots.

You demand silence, call it respect,
But my voice is not yours to neglect.
A right so sacred, yet trampled in fear,
Your anger won't mute what you refuse to hear.

Opinions are not shackles, they're wings in the air,
They don't beg for permission, they don't wait for your care.
Don't call it rebellion, don't name it a crime,
It's the pulse of my freedom, my reason, my rhyme.

So scream if you must, but I'll scream louder,
Drown out your control with words that empower.
This voice is my weapon, my fire, my pen,
And I'll wield it fiercely, again and again.

You cannot cage thought, you cannot steal sight
For opinion is freedom, and freedom is right.

16. I Chose Me

I tried burning your letters once,
thought the flames would swallow your words whole.
But somehow, they wrote themselves back,
each sentence clinging to my mind like a song I can't forget.

My playlist is all strength now,
"I'm a survivor," "I don't need a man,"
Yet somehow, every third track feels like you.
Soft. Familiar. Too close for comfort.

I threw your hoodie out once
hurled it into a corner like I was finally done.
But there it was the next morning,
draped over my chair like it still belonged there.
Like you still belonged here.

"Move on," they say.
"Find someone better."
But if I wanted *better*,

I wouldn't have fallen for *you*.

You were messy and complicated,
half in, half out
never enough to stay,
Yet always enough to linger.

One moment I'm unstoppable
loud, fearless, walking like the world owes me space.
Next, I'm sitting with my phone in my lap,
fingers hovering over your name,
wondering if maybe, you're thinking of me too.

I tell myself I'm over you.
Tell my friends I'm *so done*.
But some nights, I still hear my phone whisper
"Maybe just one text..."

You always knew how to steal the spotlight
How to make it feel like I was lucky just to stand in your shadow.
But I'm done playing small.
I'm done writing myself as your side note.

This time, I'm choosing myself.
I'll paint my lips in bold colours if I have to.
I'll laugh too loud, love too big, and build a future

That doesn't need your half-hearted presence.

Because I'm not just moving on
I'm becoming someone you'll wish you had stayed for.

17. Cramp Chronicles

Oh yay, it's here! The *monthly gift*,
Brought to me by Mother Nature's swift.
I didn't ask for this, not today,
But she rolled in anyway like, "*Namaste!*"

It starts with a cramp, oh just a tease,
Next thing I know, I'm begging on my knees.
My uterus kicks like it's in a fight,
Bro thinks it's FIFA Finals every night.

It's a horror film in my underpants,
With jump scares, blood, and angry rants.
And don't you *dare* say, "Is it that time?"
Unless you wanna meet my hormonal crime.

Then comes the fashion disaster zone,
Wearing black pants like they're a sacred throne.
White jeans? HAH. Bold move, girl ,
That's a horror movie waiting to unfurl.

Dear Mother Nature, are you bored or cursed?
Cause this monthly madness feels like the worst.
And to all the men who say "it's not *that* bad"
Come bleed for five days, then talk, you lad.

So next time someone flinches at the word "period,"
Tell them: *"Sit down, darling. It's time you got serious."*

18. Inner Flame

They told you of a devil cloaked in flame,
A fiend with horns and a dreaded name.
But genius lies in the truth you conceal,
The devil's within you, its presence is real.

No pitchfork sharp, no sulfurous smell,
It dwells in your silence, it builds its hell.
It whispers truths, nine bold and clear,
While hiding a lie you'll clutch so near.

It doesn't shout, but cracks and screams,
Breaking your conscience, distorting dreams.
It hums a tune that feeds your belief,
That your fiend is yours alone—your grief.

A seed of greed you chose to sow,
It turned to gold, a bright false glow.
You call it a dream, but truth is bare,
The devil's smile lingers there.

Dressed in black, it paints with red,
Masterpieces of lies you've fed.
It poses as a friend at the table of choice,
Yet hides deceit in its charming voice.

Every decision, a circle of blame,
Each step fuels the devil's flame.
It whispers power, wealth, and pride,
Laughing as you hollow inside.

Free lies it gives, yet a fee it takes,
For every truth, a heart it breaks.
It forces nothing, no hand, no tool,
It merely watches you play the fool.

But here's the twist, the secret known,
Paradise lies in seeds you've sown.
You hold the power, the right to decide,
Will hatred rule, or compassion reside?

The devil thrives where love's displaced,
In hearts where kindness is erased.
But souls that question, daring to fight,
Are the devil's feast, its deepest delight.

So look within, to the love you claim,
Does it heal or burn with hidden flame?

The devil's strongest where hatred hides,
But you choose the path where your soul abides.

19. A Woman's Wardrobe

Oh, keeper of chaos, stylish and blind,
hear now the cry of a closet maligned.
Not merely hinges, nor timber and glue,
but a soul suffocating in fabric you outgrew.

Birthed in oak and carved with pride,
Polished and placed by your bedroom's side.
I was once noble, empty, divine
A vault for elegance, tailored and fine.

But now? I am chaos in cotton. A mess in mohair. A museum of mayhem. Full of despair.

You cram me with cardigans still tagged and new,
buried beneath coats you outgrew in grade two.
Dresses with sequins that never saw light,
Jackets from seasons that fled with the night
Scarves that multiply like rabbits on speed,
And boots in triplets, you didn't even need.

I gasp, yes, I GASP for a pocket of air,
but you stuff in another Zara nightmare.
A crop top with feathers, a belt in lace,
even *that* pink necklace from your "glam" phase.

Do you not hear me groan in the night?
When you slam my door shut with all your might?
My hinges scream like tortured souls,
and my hangers dangle like gallows poles.
Each shelf a battlefield, socks waging war
, one missing its pair, the other on the floor.

The weight of your jeans, oh! the denim dread!
They crush my spine, I weep, I shed.
For every high-waist, every flare-leg you own
Presses against me like a cold fashion stone.
You say, "Nothing to wear," and sob at my face,
While I hold *everything* in tight disgrace.

I deserve therapy.

Or at least a proper spring clean.
Not a "quick tidy" or last-minute sheen.
I dream of space. Of hangers aligned.
Of one... just ONE section where socks are assigned.

Oh, how I envy the bookshelf's grace

, all organised spines, no lace in its face.
Or the mirror, smug in its shiny appeal,
while I choke on your fake leather heel.

So here's my final plea, dramatic and bold
before my poor hinges grow too old:
Sort me. Fold me. Set me free.
Or you'll wake one day, and it won't be me.

Just a shell of wood, warped and worn,
with shelves that sigh and doors that mourn.
My soul replaced by silent dust,
A relic of fabric, forgotten and rusted.

Your hoodie will spill like a tragic reveal,
Buttons will scatter like secrets you conceal.
And in that moment, you'll finally see
what happens when closets lose their dignity

20. Lit by Her Ancestors

She walks with a spark, a dangerous glow,
A fire that ruins, but, oh, what a show!
The ghosts of the past whisper in her ear,
"Burn, girl, burn, let them fear!"

The witches of Salem? They nod in delight.
Suffragettes cheer as she steps up to fight.
Her ancestors sigh, "Ah, she's the one,"
Then light up a match just for fun.

She sips her tea, but it's piping hot,
Scorching the tongues of those who forgot
That she is the daughter of flames untamed,
And history itself has carved out her name.

She enters a room—men start to sweat,
Regretting the patriarchy? Oh, you bet.
She smiles so sweet, but don't be deceived,
That's just the prelude to being relieved—
Of your power, your ego, your fragile disguise,

She burns with the truth and no compromise.

The fire she carries? It's fueled by rage—
From centuries trapped in society's cage.
But don't mistake it for fury alone,
It's laughter, love, a force overthrown.

So, let them run,
She'll dance in the ashes when the battle is done.
For she carries the fire of those who once burned—
And now it's their turn to watch you learn.

21. She Who Rises

She was not born with fire,
she forged it.
From slammed doors, whispered insults,
and the echo of "No" thrown like stones
at the soft skin of her becoming.

She fell, yes, she fell,
not once, not twice,
but a thousand quiet times
in bedrooms where tears made no sound,
in classrooms where her hand was never seen,
in boardrooms where her name sat in shadows
while others basked in light.

They mistook her silence for surrender.
They thought stillness meant defeat.
But beneath that stillness
was the rumbling of mountains ready to shift,
oceans gathering storms in their belly.

They called her emotional
not knowing emotions were her army.
They called her weak
not seeing how she stitched herself whole
with every tear she refused to hide.

She has died many small deaths
the death of innocence,
the death of obedience,
the death of the girl who only ever said "yes."
And yet
every death was an evolution,
every ending just a cracked cocoon.

She rises
not with fury alone,
but with an ancient grace,
with the voices of her foremothers
woven into her breath.

She rises
like the sun after the longest night,
not asking for permission
but claiming the sky as her own.

She rises,
not to conquer others,

but to return to herself
to the truth that was waiting
beneath every wound.

She who rises
is not the same as the one who fell.
She is softer in places, stronger in others
a mosaic of scars and miracles,
a testament to every time she thought
this is the end
and still,
she rose.

www.ingramcontent.com/pod-product-compliance
Lightning Source LLC
Chambersburg PA
CBHW070457050426
42449CB00012B/3020